# HEINEMANN GUIE

## INTERMEDIATE LEVEL
Series Editor: John Milne

The Heinemann Guided Readers provide a choice of enjoyable reading material for learners of English. The series is published at four levels. At *Intermediate Level*, the control of content and language has the following main features:

*Information Control*  Information which is vital to the understanding of the story is presented in an easily assimilated manner and is repeated when necessary. Difficult allusion and metaphor are avoided and cultural backgrounds are made explicit.

*Structure Control*  Most of the structures used in the Readers will be familiar to students who have completed an elementary course of English. Other grammatical features may occur, but their use is made clear through context and reinforcement. This ensures that the reading as well as being enjoyable provides a continual learning situation for the students. Sentences are limited in most cases to a maximum of three clauses and within sentences there is a balanced use of adverbial and adjectival phrases. Great care is taken with pronoun reference.

*Vocabulary Control*  There is a basic vocabulary of approximately 1,600 words. At the same time, students are given some opportunity to meet new words whose meanings are either clear from the context or are explained in the *Glossary*. Help is given to the students in the form of illustrations, which are closely related to the text.

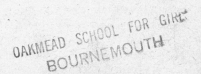

## Guided Readers at Intermediate Level

# The Great Gatsby

F. SCOTT FITZGERALD

Retold by MARGARET TARNER

*Illustrated by Kay Mary Wilson*

HEINEMANN EDUCATIONAL BOOKS
LONDON

Heinemann Educational Books Ltd
22 Bedford Square, London WC1B 3HH

LONDON EDINBURGH MELBOURNE AUCKLAND
HONG KONG SINGAPORE KUALA LUMPUR NEW DELHI
IBADAN LUSAKA NAIROBI JOHANNESBURG
EXETER (NH) KINGSTON PORT OF SPAIN

ISBN 0 435 27059 1

*The cover photograph by kind permission of
Paramount Pictures Corporation.*

Printed and bound in Great Britain by
Richard Clay (The Chaucer Press) Ltd
Bungay, Suffolk

# Contents

## Note on Difficult Words

Some difficult words and phrases in this book
are important for understanding the story.
Some of these words are explained in the story,
some are shown in the pictures, and others are
marked with a number like this . . .[3]
Words with a number are explained in the
Glossary on page 64.

# Introduction

My name is Nick Carraway. I was born in a big city in the Middle West[1]. My family has been well-known there for seventy years. My father's university was Yale and I went there too. I graduated[2] in 1915 and then went to fight in the Great War.

When I came back from the War, life in the Middle West was dull. I could not settle down[3]. I decided to go East and learn the bond business[4]. My father agreed to pay my expenses for the first year. So, in 1922, I went to New York. I had planned to stay in the East for several years, but I was there for only one summer. This book is the story of that summer.

I arrived in New York in spring. The weather was already warm and the city was hot and uncomfortable. I looked around for somewhere cheap to live. I found a little house about twenty miles from New York, near the village of West Egg.

My house was on Long Island, near the sea. It stood between two enormous[5] houses that had been built for millionaires. The house on the right of my house had a swimming pool and was surrounded by beautiful lawns and gardens. It was Gatsby's house. And this is Gatsby's story, but of course, I didn't know Gatsby then . . .

# 1. Tom and Daisy

That spring, the sun shone every day. I was lonely at first in the East. But I felt that this was the real beginning of my life. I walked in the fresh air. I bought books. I worked hard. I was trying to make myself a successful business man.

One evening, the phone rang. It was my cousin Daisy.

'Hallo, Nick,' she said in her soft voice. 'Do you know we are neighbours? Tom and I are living across the bay[6], in East Egg. I think we've settled down at last. Do come to dinner, Nick. I'd love to see you.'

Of course, I agreed. I wanted to see my cousin Daisy again. She had married Tom Buchanan, a man I had known at Yale University. Tom had been a famous football player at college. His family was very rich and Tom had spent money carelessly. Now he and Daisy had left Chicago, where I had last seen them. After the War, they had travelled around America and Europe. I did not believe they had really settled down. They were too rich and too restless[7].

So, a few days later, I drove over to East Egg. The Buchanans' house was a big one, overlooking the bay. The lawns and gardens started at the house and went down to the sea. It was late afternoon and the weather was warm and windy. All the windows at the front of the house were wide open.

Tom Buchanan stood on the porch[8], his legs wide apart. He was a fair-haired man of about thirty. He wore smart riding-clothes[9] and his body looked strong and cruel.

We talked for a few minutes on the sunny porch.

'I've got a nice place here,' Tom told me. He took hold of my arm and showed me the outside of the house. Then we looked at the rose-garden and walked down to the sea. There was a big motor-boat at the end of the dock[10].

'Come inside now and see Daisy,' Tom said.

We walked into the house and into a high room with windows at either end. The windows were open and the wind blew the curtains up towards the ceiling, then down towards the thick carpet.

Two young women were sitting on an enormous couch[11]. Their white dresses blew about in the wind until Tom shut the windows.

The younger girl on the couch was Miss Baker. The other girl was my cousin Daisy. Daisy leaned forward and gave a charming[12] little laugh.

'I'm so very happy to see you again,' Daisy said. Her eyes were bright and exciting, but her smile was sad. I told Daisy that I had stayed in Chicago on my way to New York. Lots of friends had sent her their love.

'That's wonderful,' Daisy cried. 'Let's go back, Tom. Tomorrow!'

'I'm staying here, in the East,' Tom said firmly. 'I'll never live anywhere else.'

At that moment, drinks were brought in. Miss Baker did not take one.

'No thanks,' she said. 'I'm in training[13].'

Tom looked at her in surprise.

'You are?' He took his drink and drank it quickly. 'I don't know how you get anything done.'

I looked at Miss Baker and wondered what she did. She was slim, with grey eyes and a pale, unhappy face. I was sure I had seen her before.

'You live in West Egg,' Miss Baker said to me. 'I know somebody there. Gatsby. You must know Gatsby.'

'Gatsby?' Daisy asked quickly. 'What Gatsby?'

Before I could answer, we were told that dinner was ready. Tom Buchanan led[14] me from the room. We were dining outside, on the porch. Four candles were burning on the table.

'Why candles?' said Daisy, putting them out. 'It's not dark enough for candles.'

4

Miss Baker sat down at the table and yawned.

'We ought to do something,' she said in a tired voice.

'All right,' said Daisy. 'What shall we do? What do people do, Nick?' she asked me.

When dinner was nearly over, the phone rang in the house. The butler[15] came out and said something quietly to Tom. Tom stood up without saying anything and went inside. Daisy smiled at me across the table. Then she suddenly stood up and walked quickly into the house. Miss Baker leaned forward in her chair.

'Mr Gatsby is my neighbour,' I began.

'Shhh . . . ! Don't talk. I want to see what happens,' Miss Baker said.

'Is something happening?' I asked.

'Don't you know?' Miss Baker said. 'Tom's got a woman in New York. I thought everyone knew. But she shouldn't phone him at home, should she?'

At that moment, Daisy and Tom came back together.

'So sorry we had to leave you,' Daisy said.

The candles were lit again. We sat for a while in silence, finishing our wine. Then Tom and Miss Baker walked back into the house. Daisy put her elbows on the table and rested her head in her hands.

'We don't know each other very well, Nick,' she said softly. 'You didn't come to my wedding.'

'I wasn't back from the War.'

'That's true. Well, Nick, I've had a very bad time. I don't really care about anything any more. Shall I tell you what I said when my daughter was born?'

'Do.'

'Well, when I knew I had a girl – I cried. Then I was glad. I hope she'll be a fool. That's the best thing for a girl to be, a beautiful little fool. I think life's terrible, Nick. I've been everywhere and done everything. And I hate it all!'

When Daisy was speaking, I believed her. I felt sorry for her too. Then I saw an unpleasant little smile on her lovely face and I knew she had not been telling the truth.

Inside the house, Tom and Miss Baker were sitting on the long couch. She was reading aloud from a magazine and the light shone on her golden hair.

As Daisy and I came in, Miss Baker threw down the magazine and stood up.

'It's ten o'clock,' she said. 'Time for me to be in bed.'

'Jordan's playing in the big golf match tomorrow,' Daisy explained.

'Oh, you're Jordan Baker,' I said. I had seen her picture in the newspapers. I had heard a story about her too – how she had behaved badly in a golf match.

'Good night, Mr Carraway,' Jordan said softly. 'I'll see you again sometime.'

'Of course you will,' said Daisy. 'I think I'll arrange your marriage. I'll always invite you together and . . .'

'Good night,' Miss Baker called from the stairs. 'I haven't heard a word.'

'She's a nice girl,' said Tom after a moment, 'but she shouldn't travel round the country alone.'

'But Nick's going to look after her now, aren't you, Nick?' said Daisy. 'Jordan's from my home-town, Nick. We grew up together.'

Tom looked hard at Daisy.

'Have you been telling Nick secrets?' he asked.

'Have I?' said Daisy, smiling at me. 'What did we talk about, Nick? I can't remember.'

'Don't believe everything she tells you, Nick,' Tom said.

A few minutes later, I went home. Tom and Daisy came to the door and stood there together. Two rich people, with everything they wanted. But Daisy had told me she was unhappy. And Tom had a woman in New York.

When I got back to West Egg, I sat for a while outside my house. In the bright moonlight, a cat moved silently across the garden. As I turned my head to watch it, I saw that I was not alone. Fifty feet away, someone was standing on the lawn of Gatsby's house. The man stood very still, his hands in his pockets. I was sure it was Mr Gatsby himself.

I almost called out to him. But he seemed happy to be alone. He slowly stretched out his arms to the dark water. I looked out to sea too. There was one green light, very small and far away.

When I looked back to Gatsby again, he had gone. I was alone now in the dark night.

## 2. Myrtle Wilson

About half way between West Egg and New York, the railroad[16] crosses a dirty, narrow river. Trains always wait there. It was because of this that I met Tom Buchanan's mistress[17] for the first time.

One Sunday afternoon, Tom and I were going up to New York by train. I could see that Tom had been drinking. When we got to the river, the train stopped as usual. A dusty road ran by the side of the railroad. It was an ugly place.

Suddenly, Tom stood up and took my arm.

'Come on,' he said. 'I want you to meet my girl. Jump down!' And he pulled me off the train, on to the dusty road. I followed Tom to the only building in sight. There were three shops in the building and one was a garage. The sign said –

*Repairs*   GEORGE B. WILSON   *Cars bought and sold*

Tom and I went into the garage. There was one dusty old car in the corner. As I was looking around in surprise, a thin man came out of the office.

'Hallo, Wilson, old man[18],' Tom shouted. 'How's business?'

'Not bad,' said Wilson unhappily. 'When are you going to sell me that car?'

'Next week. My driver's working on it now.'

'He works slow, doesn't he?' said Wilson.

'No, he doesn't. And if you feel like that, I can sell it to someone else,' Tom said angrily.

'I don't mean that,' said Wilson. 'I . . .'

His voice stopped. I heard footsteps on the stairs. Then a woman was standing in the doorway.

She was in her middle thirties. She was not beautiful, but her face and body were full of life. She smiled slowly and walked past her husband. She shook hands with Tom and looked into his eyes.

'Why don't you get some chairs, George, so everyone can sit down?' she said.

'All right,' said George Wilson hurriedly and he went towards the little office.

'I want to see you,' Tom said quickly to the woman. 'Get on the next train. I'll meet you in New York.'

'All right.'

She moved away. George Wilson came out with two dusty chairs. But Tom had already turned to go.

*    *    *    *

'It's good for Myrtle to get away,' Tom said as we were waiting for the next train.

'Doesn't her husband care?'

'Wilson? He thinks she goes to New York to meet her sister. He's a fool.'

And so Tom Buchanan, his girl and I went up to New York. But Mrs Wilson sat in another part of the train. On the station at New York, she bought magazines and perfume. We all got into a taxi. Almost at once, Mrs Wilson

told the the driver to stop. An old man was standing by the road side with a basket of puppies.

'I want one of those dogs,' Mrs Wilson said. 'It will be nice to have one in the apartment[19]. What kind are they?' she asked the man. 'I want a police dog.'

The old man looked into the basket.

'I got all kinds, ma'am,' he said, pulling out a puppy.

'That's not a police dog,' said Tom.

'No,' said the old man.

'I think it's cute[20],' said Myrtle Wilson. 'How much is it?'

'Ten dollars, ma'am.'

'Here's your money,' said Tom impatiently to the man. 'You can get ten more dogs with it.'

We drove over to Fifth Avenue[21] and I tried to leave them there.

'No, you don't,' said Tom quickly. 'Myrtle wants you to see the apartment, don't you, Myrtle?'

'Sure[22],' Myrtle Wilson said. 'I'll phone my sister, Catherine. People say she's beautiful.'

So we drove on until we came to the apartment house. Myrtle Wilson got out of the taxi like a queen.

'I'm going to ask the McKees to come up,' she said in the elevator[23]. 'They live in the apartment below. And I'll phone my sister, too, of course.'

The apartment was four small rooms on the top floor. The living-room was crowded with furniture. Mrs Wilson sent the elevator boy[24] out to buy food for the dog. Tom took a bottle of whisky from a locked cupboard.

I have been drunk only twice in my life. The second time was that afternoon. I remember Myrtle Wilson sitting on Tom's knee. After a time, I went out to buy some cigarettes. When I came back, the living-room was empty. So I sat there smoking and reading the magazines. Just as Tom and Myrtle came out of the other room, the sister, Catherine, arrived. She was about thirty, thin and red-haired with a white face. Then the McKees came up from the apartment below.

Myrtle Wilson had changed her dress. It was very tight and looked expensive. Her laughter, and the way she moved had changed too. She spoke and walked like a rich, fashionable woman.

'I like your dress,' said Mrs McKee.

'This old dress? I've had it for years,' Myrtle laughed.

'Have something to drink,' Tom said to the McKees. 'Get some more ice, Myrtle, before everyone goes to sleep.'

'I told the boy about the ice,' Myrtle said angrily. 'These people! You have to tell them all the time.'

Myrtle's sister, Catherine, sat down beside me on the couch.

'Do you live down on Long Island too?' she asked me.

'I live at West Egg.'

'Really? I was at a party there about a month ago. At the house of a man called Gatsby. Do you know him?'

'I live next door to him.'

'Do you? He's awfully rich, you know. People say he got his money from Germany. In the War. I'm afraid of him.'

Catherine moved closer and looked across the room at Tom and Myrtle.

'Both of them are unhappily married,' she said. 'But Tom's wife is a Catholic. She won't divorce[25] him.'

I knew this was untrue and I was shocked.

'Why did you marry Wilson, Myrtle?' Catherine called across the room. 'Nobody made you do it.'

Myrtle laughed.

'Well, I thought he was a gentleman. I must have been crazy!'

Tom now sent the elevator boy to buy some sandwiches and a second bottle of whisky. I wanted to go home. I went to the window and looked down into the dark street. Were people looking up at our lighted window and wondering what was going on?

Myrtle Wilson called to me to sit down again. She began to tell me about her first meeting with Tom.

'It was on the train,' she said. 'We couldn't stop looking at each other. When we got to New York, we got into a taxi together. I was so excited that I couldn't see where we were going. But I didn't care. You can't live for ever, you know. You can't live for ever.'

The room was filled with Myrtle's loud, false[26] laughter. She turned to Mrs McKee.

'My dear,' Myrtle said, 'I'm going to give you this dress. I'm getting another tomorrow. I've got so many things to buy: a collar for the dog, an ash-tray . . . And I must go to the hairdresser's.'

It was nine o'clock. Then I looked at my watch again – it was ten. The room was full of smoke. People were coming and going, shouting to each other across the room.

At about midnight, Tom and Myrtle started to argue.

'Daisy! Daisy! Daisy!' Myrtle Wilson was shouting. 'I'll say her name whenever I want to. Daisy! Dai . . .'

With a short hard movement, Tom Buchanan hit her across the nose. Myrtle cried out with pain. Someone got towels. Then the towels, covered with blood, were all over the floor. People were screaming and shouting. Myrtle Wilson lay on the couch. Her nose was still bleeding and she was crying loudly.

Mr McKee woke up and walked towards the door. I picked up my hat and followed him out. We went down in the elevator together.

Then I was on the station, half-asleep, waiting for the early morning train to West Egg.

# 3. I Meet Gatsby

My neighbour, Mr Gatsby, gave parties all through the summer. Nearly every night his house and gardens were full of music. Men and women walked among the beautiful flowers, laughing, talking and drinking champagne[27].

In the afternoons, Gatsby's guests[28] swam in the sea or sat on his beach. His motor-boat roared across the bay. Every week-end, Gatsby's cars carried his guests to and from the city.

Coloured lights hung from the trees in Gatsby's gardens. Food was brought from New York – rich, beautiful food – and it was put on long tables under the trees. There was every kind of drink.

At seven o'clock, the band started to play. Cars from New York were parked outside Gatsby's house. Soon, everyone was a little drunk and talking to people they had never met before.

As it became dark, the lights grew brighter. The music and laughter were louder now. More and more people arrived. A girl began to sing with the band. The party had started!

Not all these people had been invited to Gatsby's house. All kinds of people drove out to Long Island and stopped outside Gatsby's door. Then they joined the party and started to have a good time. Sometimes they were introduced to Gatsby. Sometimes they never saw him.

One day, I was invited to one of Gatsby's parties. As soon as I arrived, I began to look for Gatsby to thank him for his invitation. But no one knew where he was.

As I went to get a drink, I saw Jordan Baker. I walked towards her, glad to see someone I knew.

'I thought you might be here,' Jordan said.

We took our drinks and sat down at a small table under a tree. Jordan began to talk to a girl in a yellow dress.

'Do you come to these parties often?' Jordan asked her.

'I come here when I can,' the girl said. 'No one cares what I do, so I always have a good time. Last time I was here, I tore my dress. Do you know, Gatsby sent me a new one! It cost him 265 dollars!'

'There's something strange about a man like that,' another girl said. 'He doesn't want any trouble from anybody.' She leaned across the table and said, 'Somebody told me that Gatsby killed a man!'

'I heard he was a German spy,' a man added.

'Oh, no, he was in the American army in the War. But I'm sure he's killed a man!' someone else said. And the girls laughed excitedly.

Supper was now being served. Jordan and I left our table and went to look for Gatsby.

The bar in the garden was crowded, but Gatsby wasn't there. We walked into the house, opened a door and found ourselves in a library. A fat, middle-aged man was leaning against the table. He stared at us through his round glasses.

'What do you think?' he asked, 'all these books – they're real[29]!'

'Are they?'

'Sure. I thought they were made of cardboard. Here, look! Gatsby is smart[30], he does everything right!' And the man held up a book in front of our faces.

'How did you get here?' the fat man asked. 'I was brought. I've been drunk for a week.'

He shook hands with us and smiled. Jordan and I left him and went back into the garden.

People were dancing now. The voices and the laughter were very loud. The moon was high in the sky. Champagne was being served in big glasses.

Jordan and I sat down at a table with a well-dressed man of my own age. I was enjoying myself now. The music stopped for a moment. The man at our table looked at me and smiled.

'I think I know your face,' the man said. 'Weren't you in France during the War?'

'Yes, I was.'

'Me too,' he said. We talked about the War for a few minutes. Then the man told me that he had a new motor-boat.

'Want to go out with me in the morning, old sport[31]?' he asked.

'Sure, what time?'

'Let's say nine o'clock.'

I looked around the garden and smiled.

'This is an unusual party,' I told the man. 'I haven't seen my host[32] yet. Gatsby sent me an invitation this morning. I ought to thank him.'

The man stared at me in surprise.

'I'm Gatsby,' he said. 'I thought you knew, old sport. I'm not a very good host, am I?'

Gatsby smiled. He had a pleasant smile. His smile made me feel important. I looked at Gatsby with interest. He was a tough-looking young man, but he had beautiful clothes and beautiful manners.

At that moment, the butler hurried up to our table. Gatsby stood up and bowed to each of us.

'Chicago's on the phone, you must excuse me,' he said politely. 'Please ask for anything you want, old sport. I will see you again later.'

When Gatsby had gone into the house, I said, 'Who is he, Jordan? Does anyone know?'

'He's a man called Gatsby. That's all I know.'

'But where is he from? What does he do?'

'Now you've got interested in him,' Jordan smiled. 'Everyone does. He told me once he was educated at Oxford, England. But I don't believe it.'

'Why not?'

'I don't know. But who cares? He's got good manners and he gives big parties. I like big parties.'

There was a crash on the drums and the band-leader spoke.

'A new jazz tune for Mr Gatsby,' he cried.

The band began to play. I looked up and saw Gatsby standing alone on the white steps in front of his house. His face was tanned[33] and his hair was cut short. Gatsby stood there, very straight, his hands in his pockets. I wondered why people seemed a little afraid of him.

When the jazz tune ended, every girl kissed the nearest man and fell into his arms, half-drunk. But there was no girl in Gatsby's arms. He stood there, on the steps, alone.

The butler came back to our table.

'Miss Baker,' he said, 'Mr Gatsby would like to speak to you.'

'To me?' Jordan got up slowly and walked into the house.

It was almost two o'clock now. Someone was singing. I went into the house to listen. A tall woman was standing by the piano, very drunk. As she sang, she cried. Suddenly, she dropped her glass and fell back into a chair, fast asleep.

It was time to go home. As I walked towards the door, Jordan Baker and Gatsby came out of the library together.

'I've heard the most surprising thing,' Jordan told me quietly. 'But I can't tell you about it – it's a secret!' She yawned. 'I must go. My friends are waiting. Do phone me.'

A few guests were standing near Gatsby. I went up to him to say goodbye.

'Don't forget we're going out in the boat, old sport,' he said. 'At nine o'clock.'

Then the butler said,

'Philadelphia wants you on the phone, Mr Gatsby, sir.'

'All right, wait a minute.'

Gatsby smiled at me.

'Good night, old sport, good night.'

I walked down the steps. The lights of a dozen cars shone on the gardens. Drunken voices were saying good night.

I walked across the lawn in the moonlight. The cars drove away. The gardens were quiet and empty.

All alone, Gatsby stood on the white steps, waving goodbye.

## 4. I Have Lunch With Gatsby

I worked hard that summer. I met a lot of business people and began to understand my job. I enjoyed living in the East. I liked New York and its crowds of people.

I didn't see Jordan Baker for a while. Then, about midsummer, we met again. Was I in love with Jordan? I don't think so, but I enjoyed being with her.

Gatsby went on giving parties and Jordan and I went to some of them. All the most fashionable people went to Gatsby's parties. They came to Gatsby's house, drank his wine and told each other crazy stories about him: 'He's a bootlegger . . . a crook . . . a gambler . . .[34] he's killed a man . . .'

All these things were said about Gatsby. But no one knew the truth about him. And, while he went on giving parties, no one cared.

One morning, late in July, Gatsby's car stopped outside my door. It was the first time Gatsby had called on me.

'Good morning, old sport,' he said. 'You're having lunch with me today. We can drive up to New York together.'

Gatsby got out of his beautiful yellow car and stood beside it proudly.

'It's pretty, isn't it, old sport?' he said. 'Have you seen it before?'

Of course I'd seen it. Everyone in West Egg knew

Gatsby's car. Yellow and silver, it shone in the morning sun. We made ourselves comfortable on the green leather seats and set off for New York.

I hadn't talked much to Gatsby before. I was interested in him, but I knew very little about him. As he drove along, Gatsby didn't say anything at first. Then suddenly he spoke.

'Look here, old sport,' he said, 'what do you think of me?'

Before I could answer, Gatsby went on, 'You must have heard a lot of stories about me. Well, now you're going to hear the truth. I'm the son of rich people in the Middle West – they're all dead now. I grew up in America, but I was educated at Oxford. All my family went there.'

Gatsby looked at me for a moment. He was talking quickly and I didn't believe a word he was saying.

'What part of the Middle West are you from?' I asked.

'San Francisco.'

'San Francisco? But that's not . . .'

'My family died,' Gatsby went on in a slow, sad voice. 'After that, I lived all over Europe. I travelled, collected jewels, hunted animals . . . I was spending money to forget something very sad.'

I was so sure now that Gatsby was lying, that I almost laughed.

'Then the War came, old sport,' Gatsby said. 'I was glad. I tried to die, but I couldn't. I was a success. I won medals[35]. Look, here's one of them.'

Gatsby took a medal out of his pocket. I looked at it in surprise.

'Major Jay Gatsby,' I read, 'for Valour Extraordinary[36].'

Then Gatsby took out a photograph.

'I always carry this, too. Taken at Oxford.'

In the photograph, some young men were standing outside a college gate. I recognised Gatsby. Was he telling the truth then?

'I'm going to ask you a favour[37],' Gatsby said, putting the photograph away. 'That's why I've told you about myself. You'll hear more this afternoon.'

'This afternoon?'

'Yes, when you have tea with Miss Baker. I've asked her to speak to you . . . about a certain matter.'

Gatsby drove faster. As we passed Wilson's Garage, I saw Myrtle Wilson selling gas[38].

We raced on towards the bridge. There was New York on the other side of the river. I felt excited, as I always did, when I saw the city.

'Anything can happen in New York,' I thought, 'anything. I can even believe Gatsby's story!'

$$*\qquad*\qquad*\qquad*$$

At noon, I left work to go to the restaurant where I was having lunch with Gatsby. He was already there, talking to a small dark man with a large head.

'Mr Carraway,' Gatsby said, 'this is my friend, Mr Meyer Wolfsheim.'

Gatsby led us to a table and ordered drinks.

'This is a nice restaurant,' said Mr Wolfsheim, looking round. 'But the place across the street is better.'

'What place is that?' I asked.

'The old Metropole,' Mr Wolfsheim said sadly. 'I remember the night they shot Rosy Rosenthal over there. Shot him four times and then drove away . . . Poor Rosy, he was a good friend of mine.'

The food arrived and Mr Wolfsheim began to eat greedily. All the time he was eating, he was watching everyone in the room. Gatsby suddenly looked at his watch. He stood up and hurried out.

'He has to phone,' said Mr Wolfsheim. 'He does a lot of business with Chicago. Gatsby's a fine fellow, isn't he? Good looking, and a perfect gentleman[39]. He's an Oxford man, you know.'

23

'Oh, is he? Have you known Gatsby for long?' I asked.

'Several years,' Wolfsheim answered. 'I met him after the War. He comes from a good family. He's a gentleman to everyone, especially women. He'd never look at another man's wife.'

When Gatsby came back to our table, Mr Wolfsheim got to his feet and looked round the room.

'I have enjoyed my lunch,' he said, 'but I've got to leave you two young men now.' And he hurried away.

'Wolfsheim's well-known on Broadway[40],' Gatsby told me

'Who is he then – an actor?'

'No, Meyer Wolfsheim's a gambler. He's clever, but he's done a lot of dangerous things.'

'Has he ever been in jail?'

'They can't prove anything, old sport. He's too smart.'

It was time to go. As we stood up, I saw Tom Buchanan on the other side of the crowded room. When he saw me, Tom came over.

'Where've you been?' he asked me angrily. 'Daisy wants to know why you haven't phoned.'

'This is Mr Gatsby, Mr Buchanan,' I said.

The two men shook hands without speaking. There was a strange look on Gatsby's face.

'How are you?' Tom asked me. 'And why are you eating here?'

'I've been having lunch with Mr Gatsby . . .'

And I turned to speak to Gatsby, but he had gone.

# 5. Daisy and Gatsby: The Start of the Dream

Later that afternoon, I met Jordan Baker at the Plaza Hotel. After tea, she told me that Gatsby had known Daisy. They had known each other in the Middle West five years before.

'Daisy and I grew up in the same town,' Jordan began. 'In 1917, Daisy was eighteen. She was the most beautiful and the most popular girl in Louisville. Her family was very rich. Daisy always dressed in white and she had a little white car. She went out with all the young officers. The telephone in her house rang all day long.

'One day in October, I was walking past Daisy's house. Daisy was sitting in her car with an officer I hadn't seen before. They were so busy talking, that they didn't see me. But I remember the way the young officer looked at Daisy. To him she was the most beautiful thing in the world.

'About a month later, Daisy's mother found her packing her bag to go to New York. Daisy wanted to say goodbye to an officer who was going overseas. Her family stopped her, of course.'

'Was the officer Gatsby?' I asked.

'Of course,' said Jordan. 'Daisy was sad for a time and didn't go out much. By the following autumn, she was gay again. In February, she got engaged to a young man from New Orleans. But in June, she married Tom Buchanan from Chicago. It was the biggest wedding our town had ever seen.'

'Were you there?' I asked.

'I was a bridesmaid[41],' Jordan said. 'On the day before the wedding, Tom gave Daisy some pearls, worth 350,000 dollars. That evening, Daisy's family was giving a big dinner.

'Half an hour before the dinner started, I went up to Daisy's room,' Jordan went on. 'The pearls were on the

floor. Daisy was lying on the bed with a bottle of wine in one hand and a letter in the other. She was very drunk.'

' "Never had a drink before," Daisy said, "but how I enjoy it!" She picked up the pearls and said, "Here, take them downstairs. Tell them Daisy's changed her mind." Then she began to cry. She cried and cried. I found her mother's maid and we got Daisy into a cold bath. The letter in her hand came to pieces in the water. Half an hour later, Daisy walked downstairs. She looked very beautiful and the pearls were round her neck.

'Next day, Daisy married Tom Buchanan and they went on their honeymoon. I met them again when they came back. I've never seen a girl so in love with her husband. That was in August.

'A week later, Tom crashed his car. The girl with him broke her arm and the story got into the papers. The girl was a maid from the hotel.

'The following April, Daisy had a baby girl and the family went to France for a year. Then they went back to Chicago.

'Well, about six weeks ago, I asked you about Gatsby,' Jordan went on. 'Daisy heard me. She knew he was the same man she had known in Louisville.'

'It's strange that Gatsby came East too,' I said.

'But it isn't strange at all,' Jordan replied. 'Gatsby came here to be near Daisy. He can see her house across the bay.'

Then there was a reason for all those parties. Gatsby had hoped that one evening Daisy would walk into his house.

'Gatsby wants you to do something for him,' Jordan was saying. 'He wants you to invite Daisy to tea. Then he'll call in too. He wants to show Daisy his house.'

I thought for a moment. Gatsby wasn't asking very much. He had waited five years. He had given big parties to strangers. And why? To see Daisy, one afternoon, at tea.

'Does Daisy want to meet Gatsby again?' I asked.

'Oh, she doesn't know about it,' Jordan answered.

'Gatsby wants it to be a surprise.'

It was dark outside by now. I asked Jordan out to dinner and we took a taxi. It was a beautiful night.

I had heard enough about Daisy and Gatsby.

I put my arm around Jordan, looked into her grey eyes and kissed her.

# 6. Daisy Comes to Tea

It was nearly two o'clock in the morning when I got home. For a moment, I thought my house was on fire. Then I saw that all the lights were on in Gatsby's house. But everything was silent. There was no music and no happy laughter.

As I stood there, Gatsby walked across the lawn towards me.

'I thought it was a party,' I said.

'No, I'm all alone, old sport. Why not come for a drive in my car?'

'It's too late.'

'Well, what about a swim? I haven't used the pool all summer.'

'I've got to go to bed,' I said.

'All right, old sport.' But Gatsby did not move. I knew what he wanted to ask me.

'I've had a talk with Miss Baker,' I said. 'I'll phone Daisy tomorrow. What day would be best?'

'I don't want to put you to any trouble . . .' Gatsby began quickly.

'How about the day after tomorrow?'

'Fine,' Gatsby said. 'I must get the grass cut . . . get a few flowers. We must have everything right, old sport.'

When the day of the tea came, it was pouring with rain. Gatsby had sent a man to cut my lawn. At two o'clock, Gatsby sent over enough flowers to fill every room in my little house. An hour later, Gatsby himself arrived. He was wearing a white suit, silver shirt and gold tie. He looked pale and tired.

Gatsby sat down and tried to read. But he looked up at every sound. Suddenly he stood up and said, 'I'm going home. Nobody's coming.'

'Don't be silly,' I said. 'It's only two minutes to four.'

So Gatsby sat down again and at that moment we both heard the sound of a car.

As I opened the front door, Daisy stopped her car and got out.

'Why did I have to come alone?' Daisy said with a little smile. 'Are you in love with me, Nick?'

I took Daisy's hand and led her into the living-room. Gatsby stood there, very pale, his hands in his pockets.

For half a minute there was silence. Then Daisy gave a little laugh and said, 'I'm so very glad to see you again, Jay. It's been a long time.'

'Five years next November,' said Gatsby, staring at Daisy.

I went into the kitchen to get the tea. After a few minutes, Gatsby came after me and closed the door.

'This is a terrible mistake!' he said. 'It's too late, old sport, too late.'

'Nonsense. Go back and talk to her. You're both shy[42], that's all.'

I decided to leave them alone for half an hour. I went to the window. The rain had stopped now and the sun was shining.

When I took in the tea, I made a lot of noise. But I don't think they heard a sound.

Daisy and Gatsby were both sitting on the couch. There

were tears on Daisy's face, but she was smiling. Gatsby's face was shining with joy. Their happiness filled the room.

'Oh, hallo, old sport,' Gatsby said, as if he hadn't seen me for years. 'I want you and Daisy to come over to my house.'

'You're sure you want me to come?'

'Sure of it, old sport.'

And so Daisy saw Gatsby's enormous house for the first time.

'That's your house over there, Jay?' she cried excitedly. 'Do you live there alone? It's so big!'

'I always keep it full of famous, interesting people,' Gatsby told her.

We wandered through the gardens. Daisy admired every flower, every tree, everything she saw.

We came at last to the white steps in front of the house. It was strange to see them quiet and empty.

Inside the house, we wandered through room after room. We admired the books in the library. All the beautiful rooms were empty and silent. We went upstairs and looked at bedrooms and bathrooms, painted in pale, rich colours. Finally, we came to Gatsby's own rooms where we sat down to have a drink.

Gatsby had never stopped looking at Daisy. Once, he nearly fell downstairs. He was trying to see everything in his house through her eyes. He was like a man walking in his sleep.

'It's a funny thing, old sport,' Gatsby said slowly, 'when I see . . . I can't . . . believe . . .'

He put down his drink and opened two big cupboards. He began to take out shirts, suits, ties . . .

'I've got a man in England who buys me clothes,' Gatsby explained. 'He sends things over twice a year . . .'

The brightly coloured clothes covered the table and fell on to the floor. Silk, wool, cotton – the pile grew higher and higher.

Suddenly Daisy hid her face in the shirts and began to cry.

'I don't know why I'm crying,' she said. 'But they're such beautiful shirts, Jay. I've never seen such beautiful shirts before in all my life!'

*       *       *       *

It was getting darker now and the rain had started again. Daisy and Gatsby stood together, looking out of the window. I began to walk round the room in the half-darkness.

On Gatsby's desk was a photograph of a tough-looking old man. The man was dressed in sailing clothes.

'Who's this?' I asked Gatsby.

'That's Mr Dan Cody, old sport. He used to be my best friend, years ago. He's dead now. Dan Cody had a big yacht[43] and we sailed around together for nearly five years. He was like a father to me.'

This was one of the few things that Gatsby told me about himself that was really true. But I did not know that then.

I was going to ask Gatsby more about Mr Cody, but Daisy suddenly cried out, 'Come back here, Jay, quick!'

In the west, pink and golden clouds had formed over the sea.

'Look at that,' Daisy said softly to Gatsby. 'I'd like to put you in one of those clouds and push you around in it!'

I tried to go then, but they wouldn't let me.

'I know what we'll do,' Gatsby said. 'We'll have Klingspringer play the piano.'

Gatsby found Klingspringer. He was a young man who lived in the house. In the music-room, Gatsby turned on a lamp beside the piano. He lit Daisy's cigarette with a shaking hand. They sat down together on a couch, away from the light.

Klingspringer sat down at the piano and began to play.

33

> '*In the morning*
> *In the evening*
> *Ain't we got fun. . . .*' he sang softly.

When I went over to say goodbye to Gatsby, he had a look of surprise on his face. Gatsby had dreamed of Daisy for almost five years. Now his dream was beside him. He could not believe it.

They had almost forgotten I was there. Daisy looked up as I spoke and held out her hand. Gatsby looked up too, but he didn't seem to know me.

I went out of the room quietly, leaving them together.


## 7. Gatsby's Last Party


I didn't see or hear from Gatsby for several weeks after this. I was working hard and spending my free time with Jordan.

But this was the time when everyone was talking about Gatsby. More and more strangers went to his parties. More and more strange and crazy stories were told about him. Everyone seemed to be talking about Gatsby.

Then, one Saturday, I was invited to another of Gatsby's parties. Daisy was there too, and Tom had decided to come with her. Perhaps it was because Tom was there, but the party seemed different. There was an unpleasant, uneasy feeling about it. But all the same people were there. They were drinking champagne as usual, dancing and laughing as before.

Tom and Daisy arrived as darkness was falling. Gatsby went over to them at once. Then he took them slowly round the gardens, pointing out his most famous guests proudly.

Daisy and Gatsby danced together – I had never seen Gatsby dance before. Then they walked over to my house and sat there together for about half an hour. Tom didn't seem to care. He found a girl he wanted to talk to and the evening passed as usual.

I could see that Daisy was not happy at the party. She hated all these laughing, shouting strangers. They didn't seem to care for anybody or about anything.

By the time the Buchanans were ready to leave, Tom was in a bad temper.

'Who is this Gatsby anyway?' Tom asked as he and Daisy were waiting for their car. 'Is he a bootlegger? A crook? He knows a funny lot of people! Where does he find them? Where does he get his money from?'

'Lots of people come who haven't been invited,' Daisy said. 'He's too polite to tell them to go.'

'I'd like to know who Gatsby is and what he does,' Tom repeated. 'And I'm going to find out.'

As they got into their car, Daisy looked back at the house sadly. Gatsby was nowhere to be seen.

I stayed late that night because Gatsby wanted me to. When everyone had gone, we sat on the steps together.

'Daisy didn't enjoy herself,' Gatsby said.

'Of course she did.'

'No, she didn't have a good time. I couldn't talk to her. I felt farther away from her than ever. It's hard to make her understand.'

And then Gatsby told me what he wanted. He wanted Daisy to ask Tom for a divorce. He wanted her to tell Tom that she didn't love him – that she had never loved him. That she loved only Gatsby.

Gatsby wanted to take Daisy back to Louisville, where they had first met. Gatsby and Daisy would be married. Gatsby wanted the last five years to be completely forgotten.

Gatsby didn't seem to understand how much he was asking.

'Don't ask Daisy for too much at once,' I told him. 'You can't repeat the past.'

'Can't repeat the past?' Gatsby said in surprise. 'Of course you can! Everything's going to be the way it was before. She'll see!'

Gatsby began to talk about the time when he had first met Daisy. He told me about the first time he had kissed her. That was when Gatsby's dream had begun. And he had spent his life trying to make that dream come true.

But no woman can be turned into a dream. I could see this, but Gatsby could not. He could see no reason why he and Daisy should not be happy for ever.

## 8. The Hottest Day of Summer

It was when everyone was talking about Gatsby that his parties suddenly came to an end.

One Saturday, there were no lights in Gatsby's house or in his garden. A few cars drove up to the house, but almost immediately drove away.

I wondered what was the matter. I decided to go over and find out.

A new servant opened the door.

'Is Mr Gatsby sick?' I asked.

'No,' he said rudely.

'Well, tell him Mr Carraway called.'

'Carraway. OK,' And he shut the door in my face.

Next day, Gatsby phoned me.

'Are you leaving?' I asked.

'No, old sport, of course not. I've sent all my old servants away. Daisy comes over in the afternoons. I didn't want them to talk about her in the village. Some friends of Wolfsheim are looking after me now.'

Gatsby was phoning with an invitation from Daisy. She wanted me to have lunch at her house the following day. Jordan would be there, and of course, Gatsby too.

Daisy phoned me half an hour later. She seemed glad that I had accepted the invitation. But her voice was nervous and excited.

The next day was the hottest day of the summer. The smallest movement made you hot and tired.

I drove over to the Buchanans' house with Gatsby, in his big yellow car. Its green leather seats were too hot to touch.

The room where Daisy and Jordan were sitting was dark and cool. The two girls, both dressed in white, raised their hands lazily.

'It's too hot to move,' they said together.

Gatsby stood in the middle of the room in his elegant[44] pink suit. He could not believe that he was in Daisy's own house. Daisy watched him and gave her sweet, exciting laugh.

At that moment, Tom opened the door noisily and hurried into the room.

'Ah, Mr Gatsby! Hallo, Nick,' he said, holding out his hand to me.

'Make us all a cold drink!' Daisy cried.

As Tom left the room again, Daisy went over to Gatsby and kissed him on the mouth.

'You know I love you,' she said softly.

When Tom brought in the drinks, we all drank greedily. We had lunch in the darkened dining-room and drank a lot of cold beer.

'What are we going to do this afternoon?' asked Daisy.

'And the day after that and the next thirty years?

'Oh, it's so hot,' Daisy went on, almost crying. 'I know –

why don't we drive to New York?'

She looked across the table into Gatsby's eyes.

'Ah,' Daisy cried, in her soft, exciting voice, 'you always look so cool!'

They looked at each other as though they were alone in the room.

Suddenly, Tom Buchanan understood. His wife, Daisy, was in love with Gatsby. Tom's mouth opened a little. He looked first at Gatsby and then at Daisy.

Tom stood up.

'All right, then,' he said in a hard voice. 'We're going to to town. Let's go!'

The girls went upstairs to get ready. We went out on to the porch. 'Shall we take anything with us to drink?' Daisy called down.

'I'll get some whisky,' Tom answered.

Gatsby turned to me and said, 'I can't say anything to him in his house, old sport.'

'I think Daisy's voice told him everything,' I said.

'She's always had everything she's wanted,' Gatsby went on. 'Daisy's voice is . . . full of money,' he added.

That was it. Daisy's charm was the charm of the rich and spoilt[45].

Tom came out of the house with the whisky wrapped in a towel. Daisy and Jordan followed him, looking cool and charming in their white dresses.

'Shall we all go in my car?' said Gatsby.

'You take my car,' Tom said in a loud voice to Gatsby. 'Come on, Daisy, I'll take you in this yellow one,' he added, walking towards Gatsby's car.

But Daisy moved away from her husband.

'No, Tom. You take Nick and Jordan. We'll follow you.' And she pushed Gatsby towards the Buchanans' small blue car.

Jordan, Tom and I got into the front seat of Gatsby's car.

'Did you see that?' Tom asked us angrily. 'Where did

Daisy find a man like that?'

'He's an Oxford man,' said Jordan.

'Like hell[46] he is! He wears a pink suit!' Tom said angrily. 'I'm beginning to find out the truth about Gatsby. And it's not very pleasant.'

We were all hot and bad-tempered by now. When Tom reached Wilson's garage, he had to stop for gas.

Wilson came out slowly and stood in the hot sun. He looked very ill.

'Well, come on,' Tom shouted. 'Have I got to get the gas myself?'

'I'm sick,' said Wilson. 'I've got to get away. When can you sell me your old car?'

'Next week,' Tom said quickly. 'What about buying this yellow one? I got it last week. Why are you going away?'

'My wife and I are going West,' Wilson said. 'I'm getting her away from here. I've found out something . . .'

Tom stared at him.

'Never mind about that. What do I owe you?' he said in a hard, cold voice.

As Tom was giving Wilson the money, Gatsby and Daisy drove by in the blue car.

At the same moment, I saw Myrtle Wilson looking down at Jordan from an upstairs window.

There was a look of terrible jealousy on Myrtle Wilson's face. She thought Jordan was Tom's wife.

Tom did not see Myrtle. He was thinking about what Wilson had said. In one afternoon, Tom seemed to be losing his wife and his mistress too. He drove on, much too fast, until he was beside the blue car.

Gatsby stopped and Daisy called out, 'Where are you going? It's so hot. We'll drive around and meet you later.'

But Tom wanted to stay near Daisy and Gatsby. After some argument, we all drove to the Plaza Hotel. We took a room there so that we could have a drink. It was a crazy idea.

The room was large, but it was very hot. We opened all the windows, but it made no difference.

'Oh, it's so hot!' said Daisy. 'Why did we come here?'

'Stop talking about the heat. You make it worse!' said Tom, putting the bottle of whisky on the table.

'Why not leave her alone, old sport?' said Gatsby. 'You wanted to come, you know.'

'I don't like being called old sport,' said Tom, in a bad-tempered way. 'Where did you learn to say that?'

'If you're rude, Tom, I won't stay a minute,' Daisy said. 'Why don't you phone for some ice?'

We sat in silence, waiting for the waiter to bring the ice.

Then Tom looked at Gatsby and said, 'By the way, Mr Gatsby, you were at Oxford weren't you?'

'Yes . . . I went there.'

The waiter came in with the ice. When he had gone, Tom said, 'When were you there, exactly?'

'It was in 1919,' Gatsby replied quietly. 'I was only there for five months. American officers were able to go to an English university after the War.'

So that story was true. I was glad.

Daisy got up with a smile.

'Open the whisky, Tom,' she said, 'and I'll make everyone a drink.'

'Wait a minute,' said Tom. 'I've one more question to ask Mr Gatsby.'

'Go on,' said Gatsby politely.

'What kind of trouble are you trying to make between me and my wife?'

'Stop it, please, Tom,' said Daisy quickly.

'Why should I?' Tom shouted. 'Have I got to watch a nobody from nowhere[47] make love to my wife and say nothing?'

'Now, listen,' said Gatsby. 'I've got something to tell you, old sport.'

'Oh, please don't say anything,' Daisy said. 'Why don't

we all go home? It's too hot to argue.'

'I want Mr Gatsby to give me an answer to my question,' Tom said loudly.

'Your wife doesn't love you,' said Gatsby. 'She's never loved you. She loves me.'

'You're crazy!' cried Tom, jumping to his feet.

'It's the truth,' said Gatsby. 'We've loved each other for five years, old sport, and you didn't know!'

'I tell you you're crazy,' Tom shouted again. 'Daisy loved me when she married me and she loves me now. And I love Daisy too. I always have. She knows that.'

Gatsby walked over to Daisy and stood beside her.

'Tell him the truth. Tell him you never loved him,' he said.

Daisy looked at each one of us unhappily.

'I never loved him,' she said slowly. Then Daisy turned to Gatsby with a frightened, unhappy look in her eyes.

'Oh, you want too much, Jay!' she cried. 'I love you now. Isn't that enough?' She began to cry. 'I did love Tom once, but I loved you too.'

'You loved me too . . .' Gatsby repeated slowly.

'I can't say I never loved Tom. It wouldn't be true,' Daisy said sadly.

'Of course it wouldn't,' said Tom. 'Now I'm taking you home, Daisy.'

'You don't understand,' Gatsby said quickly. 'Daisy's leaving you.'

'Nonsense.'

'Yes I am,' said Daisy, speaking with difficulty.

'You're leaving me for a little crook!' Tom shouted. 'He's a bootlegger. He's a friend of Meyer Wolfsheim. I've been hearing all about you, Mr Gatsby! You and your friends ought to be in jail!'

I looked at Gatsby. His face was hard, with a terrible expression. I could believe then that he had killed a man. He started to talk to Daisy, quickly, excitedly. Daisy did not seem to be listening. On that hot afternoon, Gatsby's dream was slipping farther and farther away from him.

'Please, Tom,' Daisy said suddenly, 'Don't say any more. You must stop all this, please.'

Tom smiled. He knew that he had won.

'You go home, Daisy,' he said in a quiet voice. 'Go with Mr Gatsby in his car. He won't trouble you again.'

And slowly, sadly, Daisy and Gatsby had gone . . .

\*       \*       \*       \*

It was seven o'clock when Jordan and I left the hotel with Tom. As we drove back over the bridge, I remembered that it was my thirtieth birthday. I felt sad and tired.

## 9. Death in the Evening

We saw the quiet crowd of people outside Wilson's garage from some distance away.

'Look's like an accident,' Tom said. 'Wilson will have some repair work at last.'

Tom slowed down. When he saw the looks on the people' faces, he stopped the car.

Inside the garage someone was crying, 'Oh, my God, oh, my God,' over and over again.

'There's some bad trouble here!' Tom said excitedly. We got out of the car and Tom pushed through the crowd into the garage.

Myrtle Wilson's body, wrapped in a blanket, lay on a table by the wall. Her mouth was open and a little blood was coming from it. Tom stood there, looking down at her.

'Oh, my God, my God!' repeated Wilson, his hands over his face.

Tom looked round the garage slowly. He went up to a policeman who was writing in a notebook.

'What happened?' Tom asked him.

'Car hit her,' the policeman said. 'She ran out into the road and was killed at once. The car didn't stop.'

'The car was coming from New York,' said someone in the crowd. 'It was a big yellow car, going about sixty . . .'

Wilson looked up and shouted out, 'You don't have to tell me what colour it was! I know it was a yellow car all right!'

'Listen,' Tom said, going over to Wilson. 'I've just got here. That yellow car I was driving this afternoon wasn't mine, do you hear?'

Wilson took no notice.

'Let's get out,' Tom said to me and we pushed our way back through the crowd.

Tom drove on slowly at first, then faster. When I looked at him, I saw that he was crying.

'That Gatsby, the God-damned[48] coward!' Tom cried. 'He killed Myrtle. He killed her and he didn't stop his car!'

Later I heard what had happened.

Wilson had at last found out that Myrtle had a lover. She refused to tell Wilson the man's name. So Wilson had locked her in her bedroom for several hours.

Just before seven, someone had heard Myrtle cry out, 'Beat me, hit me, you dirty little coward!'

Then Myrtle had rushed out into the evening darkness. She had been shouting and waving her arms. Had she wanted the yellow car to stop?

Myrtle Wilson was killed instantly and her blood ran onto the dusty road.

\*　　　\*　　　\*　　　\*

Tom stopped his car outside his house and looked up at a lighted window.

'Daisy's home,' he said. Then he looked at me and said, I'm sorry, Nick, I should have taken you to West Egg. I'll phone for a taxi to take you home. Come in and have some supper.'

'No thanks,' I said. 'I'll wait outside.'

Jordan put a hand on my arm.

'Do come in. It's only half-past nine,' she said.

I shook my head. I was feeling tired and sick. I had had enough of the Buchanans for one day.

Jordan looked at me for a moment. Then she followed Tom quickly into the house. That was the last time I saw her.

I walked slowly down the drive to wait for the taxi by the gate.

Gatsby stepped out on to the path in front of me. His pink suit shone in the moonlight.

'What are you doing here?' I asked in surprise.

'Just standing here, old sport. Was . . . was she killed?' Gatsby asked slowly.

'Yes.'

'I thought so. That's what I told Daisy.'

'I got back to West Egg and put the car in the garage,' Gatsby went on. 'I don't think anyone saw us . . .'

I stared at Gatsby, feeling that I hated him.

'How the hell did it happen?' I asked angrily.

'Well, I tried to turn the wheel,' Gatsby began . . .

I suddenly guessed the truth.

'Was Daisy driving?'

'Yes,' said Gatsby after a moment, 'but of course, I'll say I was. Daisy was very upset when we left New York. I thought driving would calm her down.

'That woman rushed into the road just as a car was coming the other way. I think she wanted us to stop. Daisy turned towards the other car and then turned back. She was very frightened. I put my hand on the wheel, but the woman was already under the car.

47

'Daisy wouldn't stop,' Gatsby explained. 'Then she fainted and I drove home. I'm waiting here now in case Tom makes any trouble.'

'Tom's not thinking about Daisy,' I said.

Then I thought for a moment. What would Tom do if he found out that Daisy had been driving? Would he believe that Myrtle's death had been an accident?

'You wait here,' I said to Gatsby. 'I'll go back to the house and see what's going on.'

The light was on in the kitchen. Daisy and Tom were sitting opposite each other at the kitchen table.

Tom was talking and holding Daisy's hand. Daisy looked up at Tom and nodded her head. They looked as though they belonged to each other. They looked as though they were planning something.

I went back to Gatsby, who was standing where I had left him. I could hear the sound of my taxi.

'It's all quiet,' I said. 'You'd better come home with me.'

Gatsby shook his head.

'I'll wait here till they go to bed. Daisy may need me. Good night, old sport.'

Gatsby put his hands in the pockets of his pink suit. I left him standing there in the moonlight.


## 10. The End of a Dream

I slept badly that night. I had terrible, frightening dreams. Just before dawn, I heard a taxi driving up to Gatsby's house. I dressed and went over there at once.

The front door was open. Gatsby was sitting in the hall, still wearing his pink suit.

'Nothing happened,' said Gatsby sadly. 'At four o'clock, she came to the window for a moment. Then she turned out the light.'

We looked round the house for a cigarette. There was dust everywhere. We sat smoking in the darkness.

'You ought to go away,' I told Gatsby. 'The police are sure to find out the yellow car is yours.'

'Go away? Of course I can't, old sport. I must find out what Daisy wants to do.'

Gatsby began to tell me about Daisy. He told me how he had first been excited by her beauty and by her money. Gatsby had been a young man without money. And he had no hope of getting any. One October night, he and Daisy had become lovers. Then he had fallen in love with Daisy. And Daisy, a girl who had everything she wanted, fell in love with him.

Life for Gatsby became more and more unreal. He spent hours telling Daisy about his dreams for the future. And, of course, she listened to him.

Then Gatsby had to go to the War. When he came back, Tom and Daisy were on their honeymoon.

\*     \*     \*     \*

The house began to fill with the pale light of dawn. Birds began to sing in Gatsby's garden.

'I don't believe she ever loved him,' Gatsby said. 'You mustn't take any notice of what she said this afternoon. She was excited and Tom frightened her.'

Gatsby and I had breakfast together, and then we went into the garden. The air was cooler. Summer was nearly over.

The gardener came up to us and said,

'I'm going to take the water out of the swimming-pool, Mr Gatsby. The leaves will be falling soon.'

'Don't do it today,' Gatsby said. 'I haven't used that pool all summer.'

It was time for me to go to work. But I didn't want to work and I didn't want to leave Gatsby alone.

'I'll phone you,' I told him.

'Do, old sport. I suppose Daisy will phone too.'

'I suppose so.'

We shook hands and I began to walk away. Then I stopped and shouted back across the lawn,

'They're no good, Gatsby! You're better than all of them!'

It was the only compliment[49] I ever paid Gatsby. But I've always been glad I said it.

Gatsby gave me a big smile and raised his hand. His pink suit was bright against the white steps.

'Goodbye!' I called. 'Thank you, Gatsby.'

\*     \*     \*     \*

Wilson had cried for Myrtle all night. Then he began to talk to his neighbours. Two months ago Myrtle had come back from New York with a bruised face. Later, Wilson had found an expensive dog collar in Myrtle's desk.

'He bought it for her,' Wilson said. 'He bought it for her and then he killed her! He murdered her, the man in the yellow car! She ran out to speak to him and he wouldn't stop!'

Somehow, Wilson found out who owned the yellow car. At half-past two on the day after Myrtle had been killed, Wilson went to West Egg. He asked the way to Gatsby's house.

At two o'clock, Gatsby had gone down to his swimming-pool with an airbed[50]. He told his servants to call him if anyone phoned.

No one phoned. His dream was over.

I couldn't do much work that day. I got back to West Egg by about half-past four. Gatsby wasn't in the house. One of the servants told me he had not come back from the swimming-pool.

We hurried down to the pool. The airbed was moving

slowly round and round. There was a little blood in the water and Gatsby lay on the airbed – dead.

As we carried Gatsby's body up to the house, we saw Wilson lying on the grass. Wilson had shot Gatsby and had then shot himself.

*     *     *     *

At the inquest[51], Myrtle's sister swore that Myrtle had never known Gatsby. She said, too, that Wilson and his wife had been completely happy. So Wilson was called, 'a man made mad with grief[52]' and the case was closed.

*     *     *     *

About half an hour after we had found Gatsby, I phoned Daisy.

'Mr and Mrs Buchanan went away this afternoon,' a servant told me. 'They will be away for some time.'

'Did they leave an address?' I asked.

'No,' the servant replied.

'Have you any idea where they are?'

'I don't know, sir. I'm very sorry.'

I felt that I had to tell someone about Gatsby. I thought of Meyer Wolfsheim. I phoned him, but he had already left his office.

The following morning, I sent a servant to New York with a letter. Wolfsheim sent back a very short answer.

Dear Mr Carraway,

    This has been a great shock to me. I cannot go to the funeral[53] as I am very busy. I would rather not visit the house. I'll remember him as he was.

Yours truly,<br>Meyer Wolfsheim.

All that day and the next, I had to answer the questions of the police and the reporters. The news of Gatsby's death was in all the papers. But Daisy didn't phone.

Then a telegram arrived from Henry Gatz. He had read the news of his son's death in a Chicago newspaper. He was coming to the funeral.

The truth was that Jay Gatsby had started life as James Gatz. He was the son of a poor farmer in the Middle West. He had left home when he was sixteen. For a year, James Gatz had lived near Lake Superior, working as a fisherman.

Gatz had become a good-looking young man, popular with women. He had gone to college, but had only stayed there for two weeks. James Gatz was already ambitious – he was dreaming of success.

One morning, Gatz saw Dan Cody's big white yacht near the shore. Gatz found a boat and sailed over to the yacht to ask for a job.

Dan Cody asked a few questions. Gatz told Dan Cody that his name was Jay Gatsby. Cody saw that the young man with the pleasant smile was quick and ambitious. When the yacht sailed, Jay Gatsby went with it.

Gatsby stayed with Cody for five years until the old man died. Gatsby didn't get any of the old man's money. But Gatsby had learnt how the rich live. Gatsby now knew what he wanted.

\*　　　\*　　　\*　　　\*

Mr Henry Gatz was already in tears when he arrived for the funeral. He was an old man and was so upset that he could hardly stand. But when he had looked round the house, he became more cheerful.

'Jimmy did well out here in the East,' Mr Gatz said. 'This is where he made all his money. He was a good boy and he had a great future. He could have done something really good for his country. I was proud of my boy, Mr Carraway. This has been a terrible shock to me.'

54

On the day of the funeral, it rained and rained. At three o'clock, the minister arrived. Gatsby's father and I waited for the other mourners. After half an hour, the minister began to look at his watch. We waited a little longer, but nobody came.

It was raining hard when we reached the cemetery. As we walked towards the grave, I heard someone following us. It was the fat man with glasses I had seen in Gatsby's library three months before.

As we stood by the grave, I saw that Daisy hadn't sent a flower or a message.

After the funeral, the fat man said, 'I'm sorry I couldn't get to the house.'

'That's all right,' I said. 'Nobody came to the house.'

The fat man stared.

'My God!' he said, 'and hundreds of people used to go there! What friends!'

## 11. I Go Back to the West

And that is the end of Gatsby's story. After Gatsby's death, I couldn't live on Long Island any longer. I wanted to go back to the West. I wanted to go back to where we all came from. I wanted to return to the place where I felt happiest.

I saw Tom Buchanan once more in New York before I left. When he stopped and held out his hand, I put my hands behind my back.

'What's the matter, Nick?' he asked. 'Won't you shake hands with me?'

'You know what I think of you,' I answered. 'What did you say to Wilson that afternoon?'

Tom stared at me and I knew I had guessed right. Tom took hold of my arm.

'Listen,' he said. 'I told Wilson the truth. He came into our house with a gun. He would have killed one of us if I hadn't told him who owned the yellow car.

'And why shouldn't I have told him?' Tom went on. 'That Gatsby made a fool of you and of Daisy too. But he was tough and he killed Myrtle like a dog!'

There was nothing I could say. I knew the truth, but I could never tell it. Tom had done what he wanted to do – get rid of Gatsby.

Tom and Daisy were rich, careless people. They took what they wanted and destroyed[54] what they didn't need. Then they went away, leaving others to clear up the mess[55].

\*     \*     \*     \*

Gatsby's house was empty when I left, and the grass had grown very long. On my last night, I stood in the garden, thinking about Gatsby and his dream.

Gatsby had believed in his dream. He had followed it and nearly made it come true.

Everybody has a dream. And, like Gatsby, we must all follow our dream wherever it takes us.

Some unpleasant people became part of Gatsby's dream. But he cannot be blamed for that.

Gatsby was a success in the end, wasn't he?

# Points for Understanding

## INTRODUCTION

1. Nick Carraway was born in a big city in the Middle West. When he came back from the War, he decided to go East.
   - (i) Why did he decide to go East?
   - (ii) What did he plan to do there?
   - (iii) How long did he plan to stay there?
   - (iv) How long did he actually stay?
2. Where did Nick find a house?
3. Who lived in the house on the right of Nick Carraway's house?

## CHAPTER 1

1. Why did Nick think that his cousin, Daisy, and her husband, Tom Buchanan, had not settled down?
2. Who did Miss Baker think was phoning Tom Buchanan?
3. Daisy told Nick that she hoped her daughter would be a beautiful little fool.
   - (i) What reasons did she give for saying this?
   - (ii) Did Nick believe her?
4. Why was Miss Jordan Baker well-known?
5. When Nick Carraway got back home, he stood for a while on the lawn outside the house. Someone was standing on the lawn outside Gatsby's house.
   - (i) Who did Nick think it was?
   - (ii) Why did Nick not call out to him?
   - (iii) What did the man do?
   - (iv) What did Nick see far away over the dark water?

## CHAPTER 2

1. When the train stopped at the river, Tom Buchanan got off with Nick.
   - (i) Where did Tom take Nick?
   - (ii) Who did Nick meet there?
2. Myrtle Wilson joined Tom and Nick in the station at New York.
   - (i) Where did Tom and Myrtle take Nick?

(ii) What did they drink there?

(iii) What happened to Nick?

3. Myrtle's sister, Catherine, had been at a party at Gatsby's house. What did she tell Nick about Gatsby?

4. 'I've got so many things to buy . . .,' Myrtle said to Mrs McKee.

(i) What did Myrtle want to buy?

(ii) Do you think they were necessary or useful things?

5. 'At about midnight, Tom and Myrtle started to argue.'

(i) What were they arguing about?

(ii) What did Tom Buchanan do?

(iii) What did Nick do?

## CHAPTER 3

1. Lots of people came to the parties at Gatsby's house.

(i) What kind of food did they eat and what did they drink?

(ii) Had everyone who came to the parties been invited?

2. Nick Carraway was invited to one of Gatsby's parties. At the party, he heard people speaking about Gatsby.

(i) What did they say about him?

(ii) Did anyone really know anything about him?

3. After Nick met Gatsby, he asked Jordan Baker about him.

(i) What did Jordan say she knew about Gatsby?

(ii) What had Gatsby once told Jordan about himself?

(iii) Did Jordan believe Gatsby?

(iv) What did Jordan think was the important thing about Gatsby?

4. The butler came up to Nick's table and spoke to Jordan. What did the butler say to her?

## CHAPTER 4

1. People went to Gatsby's parties, drank his wine and told each other stories about him. What kind of things did they say about Gatsby?

2. Everyone in West Egg knew Gatsby's car. What colour was it?

3. Gatsby drove Nick to New York in his car. Gatsby showed Nick a photograph of himself.
    (i) What did Gatsby tell Nick about his past life?
    (ii) Where was the photograph taken?
    (iii) Did Nick believe what Gatsby told him?
4. What did Nick notice as they drove past Wilson's garage?
5. How did Nick always feel as he came into New York?
6. Nick and Gatsby had lunch with Meyer Wolfsheim. What did Gatsby tell Nick about this man?
7. Tom came over and spoke to Nick. Nick turned to introduce Tom to Gatsby. What had happened to Gatsby?

## CHAPTER 5

1. Jordan Baker had lived in the same town as Daisy. Jordan told Nick about something that had happened to Daisy when she was eighteen.
    (i) Who was the officer who had been sitting with Daisy in her car?
    (ii) What did Daisy's family do when Daisy wanted to go to New York to say goodbye to the officer?
2. On the day before Daisy's wedding, her family gave a big dinner party.
    (i) What did Jordan find when she went up to Daisy's bedroom?
    (ii) What was Daisy holding in her hands?
3. 'It's strange that Gatsby came East too,' Nick said to Jordan. What was Jordan's reply?
4. 'Gatsby wants you to do something for him,' Jordan told Nick. What was it Gatsby wanted Nick to do?

## CHAPTER 6

1. Why was Gatsby waiting for Nick when he came back home?
2. How did Gatsby feel when he was showing Daisy round his house?
3. What did Gatsby tell Nick about Dan Cody? Was Gatsby telling the truth?

# CHAPTER 7

1. 'I'd like to know who Gatsby is and what he does,' Tom told Daisy and Nick. What was Tom going to do to get the answers to his questions?
2. Gatsby told Nick what he wanted Daisy to do. What did Gatsby want her to do?
3. What advice did Nick give Gatsby?

# CHAPTER 8

1. Why had Gatsby sent all his old servants away?
2. What was the weather like when Nick drove over with Gatsby to the Buchanans' house for lunch?
3. How did Tom come to realise that Gatsby was in love with Daisy?
4. On the way to New York, Tom stopped at Wilson's garage.
   (i) Why did he stop?
   (ii) Whose car was he driving?
   (iii) What did he say to Wilson about the car?
   (iv) What did Wilson tell Tom about their plans?
   (v) Who was watching from an upstairs window?
5. What was the truth about Gatsby being a student at Oxford University?
6. Gatsby asked Daisy to tell Tom that she had always loved Gatsby and had never loved Tom. What was Daisy's reply?
7. Who drove back to West Egg in Gatsby's car?
8. That day was Nick Carraway's birthday.
   (i) How old was he?
   (ii) How did he feel about life?

# CHAPTER 9

1. Why had Wilson locked Myrtle in her bedroom?
2. Myrtle Wilson ran out on to the road and was knocked down by the yellow car and killed.
   (i) Who did Myrtle think was in the yellow car?
   (ii) Who in fact had been driving the car?
   (iii) What did Tom Buchanan tell Wilson about the yellow car?

3. 'It's all quiet,' Nick told Gatsby. 'You'd better come home with me.'
   (i) What was Nick talking about when he said: 'It's all quiet.'?
   (ii) What was Gatsby's reply?


## CHAPTER 10

1. What two things about Daisy had first excited Gatsby?
2. Did Gatsby believe what Daisy had said in the hotel room in New York?
3. 'He bought it for her and then he killed her.' Wilson told his neighbours.
   (i) Who did Wilson mean by 'he'?
   (ii) What had 'he' bought for Myrtle?
   (iii) Who did Wilson think had been driving the yellow car?
4. Nick and the servants hurried down to the swimming pool. The airbed was moving slowly round and round.
   (i) What had happened to Gatsby?
   (ii) Whose body was lying in the grass?
5. When Nick tried to phone Daisy, a servant answered the phone.
   (i) What did Nick want to tell Daisy?
   (ii) What did the servant say to Nick?
6. 'Then suddenly a telegram arrived from Henry Gatz.' Who was Henry Gatz?
7. When did James Gatz change his name to Jay Gatsby?
8. How long did Gatsby stay with Dan Cody?
9. Gatsby did not get any of Cody's money when Cody died. But what had Gatsby learned from Cody?
10. Only one man turned up to be with Nick at Gatsby's funeral.
    (i) Who was the man?
    (ii) What did he say about Gatsby's friends?


## CHAPTER 11

1. 'I knew the truth, but I could never tell it.'
   (i) Who did Tom Buchanan believe had been driving the car when Myrtle Wilson was killed?
   (ii) Why could Nick never tell Tom the truth?

2. 'Gatsby was a success in the end, wasn't he?' Nick Carraway ends his story of Gatsby with this question. What is your answer to Nick's question?

# Glossary

*A note on the 1920s*

After the Great War ended in 1918, young people in America wanted to enjoy themselves. They also wanted plenty of money. Clothes, music and ideas were all new and different. A law was passed at this time which said that people could not buy or sell alcohol. But many people broke this law. A great number of people got rich very quickly. They often broke laws to make their money. People enjoyed themselves at parties by dancing to the new jazz tunes.

At this time, New York was the most modern and fashionable city of America. People went there from all over the United States. They did what they wanted to and did not care what other people thought.

1. *The Middle West* – page 1

   The northern central part of America. Chicago is one of the big industrial cities in the Middle West. People in the Middle West worked hard and did not like modern ideas.

2. *to graduate* – page 1

   to get a degree after studying at a university.

3. *to settle down* – page 1

   to decide to live in one place.

4. *the bond business* – page 1

   Nick was going to learn about investments and insurance.

5. *enormous* – page 1

   very large.

6. *bay* – page 2

   a big curve in the coastline.

7. *restless* – page 2

   they did not want to live in one place or *settle down* (see Gloss. No. 3 above).

8. *porch* – page 2
    a raised covered place at the front or sides of a house.

9. *riding-clothes* – page 2
    clothes worn when riding a horse.

10. *dock* – page 2
    a place where a boat is tied up.

11. *couch* – page 4
    a long seat for sitting or lying on.

12. *charming* – page 4
    Daisy had a very pleasant way of talking and behaving.

13. *to be in training* – page 4
    to be practising for a competition in sport.

14. *to lead someone* – page 4
    to take someone somewhere.

15. *butler* – page 5
    the most important male servant in a big house.

16. *railroad* – page 7
    an American word for railway. A track for trains to run on.

17. *mistress* – page 7
    a woman loved by a man, but not married to him.

18. *old man* – page 8
    a friendly expression used by one man to another.

19. *apartment* – page 10
    several rooms to live in, usually on one floor of a big building.

20. *cute* – page 10
    an American expression meaning attractive.

21. *Fifth Avenue* – page 10
    a famous street in New York with many expensive shops and hotels.

22. *sure* ('to be sure') – page 10
>        an American expression meaning 'of course'.

23. *elevator* – page 10
>        the American word for lift. A machine to take people
>        from one floor to another in large buildings.

24. *elevator-boy* – page 10
>        someone who looks after the *elevator* (see Gloss. No. 23
>        above).

25. *to divorce someone* – page 11
>        to end a marriage by an agreement in law.

26. *false* – page 13
>        not honest.

27. *champagne* – page 14
>        an expensive kind of white wine.

28. *guests* – page 14
>        people invited to a house.

29. *real* – page 15
>        Gatsby's library was full of books. Some rich people
>        put the covers of many books in their bookshelves to
>        show they were well educated. But Gatsby's books
>        were *real*, they could be read.

30. *smart* – page 15
>        clever.

31. *old sport* – page 18
>        an expression like *old man* (see Gloss. No. 18).

32. *host* – page 18
>        a man who invites people (*guests* see Gloss. No. 28
>        above) to his home.

33. *to be tanned* – page 19
>        to be made brown by the sun.

34. *bootlegger . . . crook . . . gambler* – page 20
>        at this time it was against the law to make, buy or sell
>        alcohol in America. People who broke this law were

called *bootleggers*. A *crook* is someone who makes money dishonestly. *A gambler* is someone who plays games for money.

35. *medal* – page 21
    a piece of metal, shaped like a coin. It is given for bravery.

36. *Valour Extraordinary* – page 21
    unusual bravery.

37. *to ask someone a favour* – page 23
    to ask someone to do something for you.

38. *gas* – page 23
    gasolene, petrol.

39. *perfect gentleman* – page 23
    someone who has good manners and is very polite.

40. *Broadway* – page 24
    a street in New York famous for its many theatres.

41. *bridesmaid* – page 26
    when a girl gets married, her best friend is her *bridesmaid*. She stands behind the bride in church.

42. *shy* – page 30
    unable to talk or behave easily with people.

43. *yacht* – page 33
    a sailing boat.

44. *elegant* – page 38
    smartly and fashionably dressed.

45. *spoilt* – page 40
    Daisy is *spoilt* because she has always had everything she wanted.

46. *like hell* – page 41
    a strong expression meaning that you do not believe something.

47. *a nobody from nowhere* – page 42
>Tom is being rude. Gatsby had become rich when he moved East. Before this time he had been a poor man from a small town in the Middle West.

48. *God-damned* – page 46
>an expression of anger and disgust, Tom thinks Gatsby is a coward.

49. *to pay a compliment* – page 51
>to say something nice about someone.

50. *airbed* – page 51
>a mattress filled with air.

51. *inquest* – page 52
>a court which describes the cause of death. When this is decided, nothing more can be said – the *case is closed*. People are asked questions and agree or *swear* to tell the truth.

52. *a man made mad with grief* – page 52
>someone so sad and unhappy that he is driven mad.

53. *funeral* – page 52
>the ceremony when a dead person is buried – or put in their *grave* in a *cemetery*.

54. *destroy* – page 57
>to break something completely.

55. *to clear up the mess* – page 57
>to put things right again.